SHOW IT UNTIL YOU KNOW IT

SHOW IT UNTIL YOU KNOW IT

A Guide to Building Self-Confidence

Heather Martell

The Place Of H LLC
Wausau

Copyright © 2021 by Heather M Martell – The Place Of H LLC

All rights reserved. No part of this publication may be reproduced, distributed, or transmitted in any form or by any means, including photocopying, recording, or electronic or mechanical methods, without the prior written permission of the publisher, except in the case of brief quotations embodied in critical reviews and certain other noncommercial uses permitted by copyright law.

Book editor: Karen Nerison

Cover designed by: Stephanie Kohli Art LLC   stephaniekohliart.com

ISBN: 978-1-7367714-0-2

Library of Congress Control Number: 2021904682

theplaceofH.com

#H #thePlaceofH

for my Z-girl

Contents

ABOUT THE AUTHOR
xi

HEALTH MATTERS
xii

INTRODUCTION
1

Chapter 1.
THE SPOTLIGHT
3

LEADERSHIP TRAITS AND COMMUNICATION
6

VERBAL COMMUNICATION
9

WRITTEN COMMUNICATION
10

NON-VERBAL COMMUNICATION
12

LEADERSHIP TRAITS
15

Chapter 2.
SHOW IT UNTIL YOU KNOW IT
17

BELIEVING IN YOURSELF
19

WHISPER IF YOU MUST
21

TRAIN YOUR BRAIN: POSITIVITY MATTERS
22

FOCUS ON THE POSITIVE
25

MY GOALS
26

Chapter 3.
SELF-WORTH: I AM WORTHY
28

SELF-CARE: IT'S IMPORTANT
34

SELF-TALK: YOU ARE LISTENING
36

Chapter 4.
THE SPOTLIGHT AND THE STAGE
40

REFLECTION (a/k/a MIRROR TIME)
42

WHERE'S YOUR STAGE?
43

Chapter 5.
MINDSET MATTERS: BE H.A.P.P.Y.
46

HARMONY: ARE YOU IN SYNC WITH YOURSELF?
47

ATTITUDE IS MINDSET AND IT DOES MATTER
48

PREPARE YOUR SURROUNDINGS AND YOU
49

PURPOSE AND PASSION
50

YOU. JUST BE.
51

Chapter 6.
IT'S SHOW TIME!
53

WITH GRATITUDE
59

THE PLACE OF H LLC
61

ABOUT THE AUTHOR

Heather Martell is the CEO and Founder of The Place of H, where she puts her years of advocacy-based leadership to work empowering others.

Moving every three years as a globe-trotting young daughter of a military family, Heather quickly honed the ability to talk with anyone and everyone.

Possessing the talent to engage, Heather has an enthusiastic personality that generates a contagious, positive energy wherever she goes. Never afraid of a microphone, a stage, or the opportunity to advocate for others, she is an accomplished speaker, trainer, coach, wordsmith, and *Laughing Soul Yoga* instructor.

She holds a mastery level, professional certification in *Leadership and Teams* and a degree of Bachelor of Science in Healthcare Management. Her strong relationship skills led Heather to great success teaching leadership development, team building, collaboration, and conflict resolution, as well as strategies to create and maintain effective teams.

Heather's passion for coaching others to know their power and their worth is a cornerstone in her life. She currently lives in Central Wisconsin.

HEALTH MATTERS

As you begin this book, it is important for you to know I am a huge advocate for mental health and wellness.

While I write about the power of focusing on and setting a positive mindset, I do not want you to pretend your way through any trauma you are experiencing.

I passionately believe you should take care of yourself when it comes to your mental health. Please seek the resources and help you need for your mental well-being. You deserve to be cared for. Take care of yourself.

You are worth it!

INTRODUCTION

This book was originally created as a leadership development seminar to empower young leaders in high school. During my teaching, I also received terrific feedback from the adult chaperones who attended the conference, so I continued to put pen to paper.

As result of many subsequent conversations, this book was written for young leaders, young professionals, and *any* leader-in-development. Regardless of the leadership path, or how long they have been established in a career *(or not even begun)*, this book is for anyone and everyone.

My intentions are to help leaders build and strengthen their self-confidence; for them to recognize the brilliance they already have within; to know their power and their worth; and to ultimately guide them to bring forth their passionate, positive leadership to impact the world.

You are that leader and *now* is the time.

Grab a pen and a highlighter and mark up this book as you see fit. Let this guidebook help you on the new path of your leadership journey.

I believe in you! -H.

1

THE SPOTLIGHT

"Let's start at the very beginning..."

Aren't you nervous? Aren't you scared? How can you get up there in front of a crowd? I could never do what you do! Speak to everyone? Share myself with them? How do you stay so happy? How do you do it? How? How?!!

When I'm peppered with questions by folks (friends, strangers, acquaintances) asking how I am able to talk in front of any number of people, I tell them well... first, I climb the stairs to the stage.

Whatever the stage may look like: the front of a classroom, a streaming web event, one-to-one meeting, or a literal stage. I climb the stairs and with my racing heart, sweaty palms, and flushed-red cheeks, I stand tall, power walk into the spotlight, and dare to shine bright!

That's when the butterflies in my stomach laugh out loud at me. *Me!* The go-getter, bring-it-on, Type A personality, don't tell me I can't do something because then I will have to do it just to prove you wrong *woman*. She has butterflies dancing in her abdomen. I am nervous as can be! But then, I remember...

I am an Academy Award® -winning actress.
I just don't have my Oscar yet.

That's it. That's how I do what I do: *I perform. I act. I believe. I show it until I know it.* I get on stage – whatever the stage is in that moment – and I act. I act like I am unafraid of presenting, teaching, or sharing. I act like the leader I have always wanted to be and have, and I perform wholeheartedly with the best of intentions. That's not to say I am perfect in my presentation; it's to say that when I stumble *(and I will stumble)* – I will smile even bigger. Laugh at myself. Take a breath. *Catch* my breath. And *keep going*.

I act like I am ready for a job interview; for a talk with my boss or a tough talk with my family; for a presentation in front of an entire organization; for coaching two people; ready to sing in front of 15,000 people; whatever it is, I'm ready. Because if I walk and talk and act like I am ready enough times, eventually I will believe me, too. Its own my self-fulfilling prophecy: *I am ready and I've got this.*

In November of 2017, I met a brilliant new friend for lunch and was asked to teach a group of high schoolers about leadership. I would be one part of an amazing team and it was an important day. Of course, I was nervous!

What would I say? Me, who is never lacking for words – would I have the right things to say? Would they be beneficial? *Truly helpful?*

I left the lunch in deep thought, and as I drove back to my office, I suddenly saw my entire training session laid out before me. As if written on the clouds, I immediately knew what I had to share... and *Show It Until You Know It*© was born!

That December, with music and energy filling the room, I welcomed my first 16 young leaders into my classroom, and we spent two hours talking about leadership development. There was enthusiastic conversation and coaching about real-life leadership scenarios, showing it until you know it, training your brain, and always reaching for the next level of leadership.

A full day with multiple, amazing leaders pouring into the next generation of leaders... it was invigorating! Teaching leadership development to eager, goal-oriented minds was life-affirming and I wanted to reach more and more people!

Throughout this book, I am going to lead you through developing your power of positivity, training your brain in times of rehearsal so it will support you in the times you need to perform, and recognizing and acknowledging your worth through a positive mindset. *You've got this!*

This book is a culmination of a lifelong dream of authorship and a gathering of life's leadership lessons I have learned along the way. My intention with my writing is to help you grow, be empowered, and be the best possible you; to support you in making a positive impact on this world; and for you to know how truly brilliant you are!

From the first state writing contest I won in elementary

school, to the *a-ha!* moments I have witnessed in the eyes of a young leader – I am excited to share this next level of my leadership journey with you.

Join me on the leadership stage and step into the spotlight... *You've got this!*

LEADERSHIP TRAITS AND COMMUNICATION

When deciding to grow as a leader, a good first step is to take stock of your current leadership capabilities. You need to have a basic understanding of your foundation before you begin growing yourself further. Can you identify any of your leadership traits?

Here are a few examples:

Authentic – Empathy
Focus – Supportive
Integrity – Character
Emotional intelligence (EQ) – Confidence
Collaborator – Creativity
Influence – Decisiveness – Communication

If you don't know what leadership traits you have, that's alright. Make time for self-reflection and ponder your leadership abilities and opportunities to-date. Do you see where and how you lead? Do you see where you could grow? Schedule time with a mentor or a trustworthy friend and ask: *Do you see traits of a leader within me? Would you help me identify the strongest and weakest of those traits?*

A good cup of coffee or tea and a great sounding board will put you on the right track to begin your development and growth as a leader.

One leadership trait I work on daily is my communication, specifically my ability to *actively listen*. Listening intently to others in order to learn from them. Whether big or small, there is usually something to be learned when listening to another person.

Actively listening to learn – not listening to respond – that is my goal in every conversation. It is often difficult for people to pay thorough attention to the other person with whom they are speaking. Your mind focuses on a point the other person made a mere 90 seconds into the conversation and you are trying to remember your counterpoint while they finish talking. Meanwhile, you have missed the other many-faceted details from their side of the conversation. *Did you really listen to what they had to say? Did you hear them? What did you learn?*

What if the conversation you are having is on the telephone? If you are focused on the points you are trying to make, you will miss key insights from the other person. If you are a leader engaging with a member of your staff, and you miss those insights, how accurately are you leading? What if they shared a cost-saving strategy for your project and instead, you are focused on responding to the expense calculation they quoted at the beginning of the call? Are you looking at your emails or the other person while they are talking to you? *Are you actively listening?*

I have always been a note-taker, a list-maker; doodling parts of a conversation to keep my mind focused on what I am hearing and to whom I am listening. The doodling often equals great notes that can support the next phase of our conversation. If we are working on a project, active listening insures I have heard all components of the project. At the end of the call, I use those notes to summarize any outstanding items needing follow-up. *Did I hear everything asked of me? Did they hear everything I asked of them?* This helps ensure all parties in the chat are on the same page and having everyone with the same information makes it easier for results to happen.

Another leadership skill I frequently practice is *not* being the first one to speak. Dear friends and co-workers of mine will laugh at this thought. *(This skill takes constant practice and self-reminders!)* This does not mean I am always biting my tongue; it means I'm giving others a chance to have their say *first*. My lack of shyness means I typically have something to contribute to a conversation. However, my vocal extroversion might silence another brilliant mind in the room. I need to pause my verbal processing to allow someone else to shine!

What if another's lack of self-confidence is holding them back? Then, it is my turn to advocate for them, inviting them into the moment, listening to their important contribution to the conversation or meeting. Being a *great listener* showcases my leadership abilities and it will showcase yours, too.

If only one half of every conversation is being heard, then you have a failure to communicate! Effective, two-way communication is one key to great leadership and success. Success for your team members. Success for your co-workers. Success for your company. Success for *you*.

VERBAL COMMUNICATION

Human beings have several ways to communicate: through speech, writing, and other non-verbal cues. Meaning, we talk, we write, and we make faces. Ok, maybe we don't simply make faces, but I've been in meetings where there were definite eyerolls happening around the room. *(Funny but true!)* So, how do *you* communicate?

Me? I am a verbal processor. This means I talk my ideas out loud, listening to my own thoughts outside of my head, and processing them anew. (Fact: this entire book has been read out loud multiple times before publishing.)

If you and I were troubleshooting a problem for our customer, we would both bring ideas to the table. You would go first *(my active listening engaged)* and then I'd give my opinions for resolution. Speaking my thoughts out loud, it is possible for me to completely talk through my plan for resolution, find a fault within my own theory, and arrive full circle back to your idea. You can hear me process my thoughts out loud.

I liken my verbal processing to how I learn music by ear. While earning my bachelor's degree, I would read out loud the meticulous notes I wrote. The combination of my multi-colored notes and hearing myself read them would make the notes 'stick' better in my mind. If I were stumped during a test, I would read the question out loud and I could suddenly 'hear' the answer in my mind. A lot like hearing the first bars of a song and having the lyrics rush to the tip of my tongue.

On the opposite side of the verbal scale is the internal

processor. This individual has the same volume of thoughts as a verbal processor; however, they mull over their answers in their minds until they are fully ready to share. I often envy their meaningful silence.

An internal processor is not failing to respond to you nor are they blowing off the work for which you've asked. They are taking the time to respond to insure they are satisfied with their answer(s) and have fully gathered their thoughts.

As a leader, you need to know how to support and work with verbal and internal processors, and to recognize the value both types of communicators bring to the table. Don't judge or discount the verbal processor by the volume of words pouring forth. They are not talking for the sake of talking; it is literally how they process the task at hand. Contrarily, do not assume the internal processor has nothing to say or add. Do not talk over them; hold space for their process and development of their work.

Knowing your own processor type brings value to the table. Knowing how to deftly navigate all types of processors will not only embolden your team, but also bolster your communication abilities as a leader.

WRITTEN COMMUNICATION

How are your written communication skills? Depending on how you use it, the pen can be a mighty weapon, slaying the ideas of a team member; or a skilled sushi knife, filleting the words for tasty consumption.

Do you use spellcheck to verify your wording? Do you pause to review every email before you click send? Are you short and sweet in your e-request? Or do you write with a flourish of words to share not only your request but perhaps your feelings on the matter, too?

Each of us is unique in our own way. Beautiful, authentic us. Some say what you write is determined by your generation. Baby Boomers would write often in order to leave a transcribed legacy behind them. Perhaps knowing the value of the written word more poignantly than some. Gen Xers like me can be lovers of words, hanging onto the edge of a literary work of art. Crafting our own dialogue for the next generations. And my millennial friends with whom I work or mentor, write emails short and sweet without any extra-ness.

When it comes to leadership, you need to understand how your team communicates through their writing, and how your written words need to effectively convey your thoughts in return. Concise enough to not lack details needed by the reader, and flowery enough to share all of your needs for a project. You want your reader to understand your intention behind the message with no room for projecting tone onto your communique.

For example, you write:
We need to talk about the proposal you drafted.

Your team member might read that and think:
Excellent! I am ready; let's talk.

They might also think:
Oh, geez... What's wrong with what I prepared now?"

The latter is what you are trying to avoid.

You will not be able to avoid all projections on your written communication because we are our own worst inner critics *(See: Self-Talk section later in this book.)* – but you can help put at ease their negative self-talk with additional details, such as:

We need to talk about adding another section to the proposal.

The best conversation starters also begin with something positive. Starting off on the right foot with a positive element not only enhances the e-conversation, it also sets the tone for on-going communications.

It's a great start! Let's talk about adding another section to the proposal you drafted.

Wave your magic wand of a pen or keyboard, start with a positive, and enlighten the reader. Save yourself and your team members from unintended angst, keep the tone of communication positive, and pay attention to how and what you author.

Taking these extra steps can put you ahead of the game as a leader. You care enough to ensure your team has effective, two-way communication, and you are rocketing towards success!

NON-VERBAL COMMUNICATION

There will come a meeting in everyone's professional life wherein you either witness or commit eyerolls as a result of someone else's talk. As a leader, you need to be on the lookout for the eyerolls – especially if you are the talker. You need to know if someone is so wholeheartedly disagreeing with you their body simply cannot hold their eyes still.

Unless you are a dictator giving orders, there is usually time for counterpoints or questions during a meeting. *Are you actively listening?* While you are speaking are you also watching for the non-verbal cues that give insight to your audience's thoughts?

From the crossed arms and furrowed brow of Molly in the corner of the room, silently and defiantly rejecting your plan; to the relaxed smiles emanating from Susan and Marcus, who are also subtly nodding their heads in agreement with a few of your points; to the sighs of John seated on your right who is clearly bored – non-verbal cues are rampant everywhere.

Understanding this silent form of communication will give you an advantage as a leader. During the next speech you give, take a read of the room. If you see someone bored and not engaging with the topic at hand, pause. *Take a breath.* Add a pointed question if you can and ask it of them.

If they offer sound answers in true concert with the topic at hand, perhaps you *are* boring the audience. What if the topic you prepared is for a less-experienced audience? Maybe you are overly prepared and talking over the heads of your audience on a topic they've never considered, let alone had opportunity to use.

Practice reading the room of the next meeting you attend. Actively listen to the speaker while scanning the room. Who do you think is agreeing with the points being made? Anyone in obvious disagreement? Anyone bored?

Adjusting the course of your talk while you're in the middle of a presentation can take practice. In addition to peppering extra questions throughout the presentation, you could change your tone *(too cheerful? monotone? somber?)*; alter the speed of your speech *(too fast? slow?)*; make more eye contact, take a breath, pause. *Mix it up!*

Lead by your willingness to change and engage your audience. Assess yourself and calibrate. You still need to be you. It's the delivery of your presentation, or talk, the leading of your meeting – *that* is what you can recalibrate.

It's like you and three team members riding together in a car when Whitney Houston's *I Wanna Dance with Somebody*® comes on the satellite radio. You crank the volume and sing at the top of your lungs, belting out the words in your best car karaoke ever! Two others join you in the raucous fun – yet the third can be seen in the rear-view mirror, furrowing their brow.

Is it the volume? Do they have a headache? Is it the song? Not a fan? Are they remembering a break-up from their youth associated with the song?

What if it's their lack of self-confidence? What if the furrowed brow and hesitance you saw was due to their self-criticism? You can adjust the volume, ask if they are alright, or even invite them to sing along with whatever words they know. Then, re-adjust the volume once more and Belt! It! Out!

"Ohhhh! I wanna dance with somebody!"®

Yesssss! You recalibrated and kept their attention. You gave a literal invitation for them to join in and sing – and you continued on as your authentic self.

LEADERSHIP TRAITS

Here again are a few examples of leadership traits:

Authentic – Empathy
Focus – Supportive
Integrity – Character
Emotional intelligence (EQ) – Confidence
Collaborator – Creativity
Influence – Decisiveness – Communication

Can you think of any other leadership traits? Jot them down.

Which leadership trait(s) do you want to grow within yourself?

Why?

How would you rate your speaking and writing skills? Why?

How/what would you change or improve?

What are some examples of non-verbal communication cues?

Any opportunities you can think of to practice your spotting skills?

You've got this!

2

SHOW IT UNTIL YOU KNOW IT

"In order to be... one must act the way..." - *Aristotle*

Throughout the years of my own leadership development, I have devoured many great authors and absorbed speeches from great leaders. During that time, I read from more than a few who directed their audience to fake it until we make it.

I would follow their advice and it would work for a while. Until my harsh internal critic would wag her finger at me, accusing me of not being real, of being fake... So, I searched for an alternative, a more positive way to say it.

When I couldn't find a way, I wrote one:

Show it until you know it.

It is still equally self-challenging: I must show myself I have the very traits or capabilities I'm seeking until I truly know they are within me. To me, the difference between the two sayings lies in the area of self-talk and ultimately, self-confidence.

One of the key issues I have with *fake it until you make it*, is the announcement that you are fake. You have just said out loud that you are going to fake it until you make it. You have announced to the world and anyone listening that you are faking it. More importantly, you have told *yourself* that you are fake, that you are faking it.

You are always listening to you. Don't announce you are fake. It is a level of negative self-talk you don't need or want. It can hinder your growth as a leader and more importantly, it can inhibit you from being authentically, awesome you. The world needs you!

Some days showing it until you know it feels like you have drawn your lips up over your teeth and hooked them to your cheeks with clothes pins. A big ol' smile pinned there for all to see, for all to believe.

As a leader, sometimes you must put on a show when you are having a bad day. Helping others, leading others all while struggling through your own turmoil or to-do list can be challenging. But you *shine* as a leader when you make this a reality for you and your team.

An important distinction: I am a huge advocate for mental health and wellness. I do not wish for you to pretend your way through continued trauma you are experiencing. I passionately believe you should take care of yourself when it comes to your mental health. Please seek the resources and help you need for your physical and mental well-being. You are worth it!

What I am writing about is the need to push through a bad review, an angry customer call, a mentor calling you out on a position paper, or your boss taking you to task. By your example, show others how to be a great leader during those types of struggle, even if you don't yet know you're a brilliant leader. *Lead.*

Show yourself just how capable you are of shining even on the greyest of workdays. Show your team what a great leader acts like during times of heavy work. Work hard, carry your part of the workload, and show your leadership. Show it until you *and* they know it. Because there will be days of burdensome, heavy work but there will be an even greater number of days full of amazing joy, triumph, and success!

BELIEVING IN YOURSELF

On the not-so-grey days, when you are excelling, and walking, talking, and showing your leadership, I ask you:

Do you believe yourself? Do you believe in yourself?

If the answer is *no* or *maybe*, then you need to keep going and growing. *You must believe in yourself first before anyone else will believe in you.* You must believe in yourself in order to truly become the leader you and the world need.

This is one of the reasons why showing it until you know it is so important. *You* are always listening, and *you* are always watching. *You are your own captive audience!*

Whatever stage you're on – in front of a crowd or practicing in front of your bathroom mirror – *you* are the most important member of your audience. You must believe in yourself *first* before anyone else in the audience will believe in you. Believe in you and the rest will follow!

Now, grab a mirror or stand in front of one. Go on, I'll wait right here... Ready?

Ok, look yourself square in the eye, and say:
I've got this. You've got this.

Again. Repeat it with more enthusiasm this time:
I've got this! You've got this!

One more time! Louder!
I'VE GOT THIS! YOU'VE GOT THIS!!

YES! You absolutely do!
YOU'VE GOT THIS!!

Believe in *you* as much as *I* believe in you!

WHISPER IF YOU MUST

Some folks will say if you want to be great, you must talk the talk and walk the walk.

Speaking it into existence is another way of saying that. I am going to speak into existence, saying out loud all my goals and desires, and I will focus on them until they come to fruition. Speaking it into existence means every fiber of my being is listening, attuned to the goals, working towards the outcome I am striving towards.

My verbal processing self has no issue with finding enough words to help speak my goals into existence. However, there are times when the world is trying to crush my dreams; or self-doubt creeps in and the inner critic tries to unleash her cone of silence around me. That's when it's more important than ever to speak out loud my goals – even if I can only muster a whisper in the moment.

Speak it out loud – even if you can only whisper right now.

You are still listening. Remind yourself of your goals and how important they are for you and the impact you wish to make in the world. And the louder the critics become? The more frequent you need to remind yourself. Say your goals out loud and the more frequently you remind yourself, the louder your own voice will become. The more you believe in yourself – the more others will believe in you.

Have you written down your goals? Grab a piece of paper, a napkin, an old receipt and *write them down!* Your goals should have importance to you. *What is one specific task you want to accomplish this year? What leadership trait do you wish to grow within you? Do you want to attain something for you and/or your family? How do you want to make an impact?*

Your goals do not need to be anything fancy; you are not being judged by anyone. Your goals are just that: *yours*. They are not set to focus anyone else's mind but yours. They are to remind you of what you are capable of achieving and to point you towards the finish line.

When reading your goals out loud, you are teaching yourself. Like the multiplication tables you learned in elementary school – *two times two equals four* and *three times three equals nine* – repetition is key!

Repeat your goals out loud until you know them, believe in them, and every fiber of your being is working towards making them a reality. It's bringing them into existence! Even when you are not consciously focused on your goals, your mind has set a course for success and is still sailing in that direction.

Let's say one goal is to read more books.
(Congratulations! Reading this book helps with your goal! Way to go!) If you read out loud your goals every morning, you are training your brain to subconsciously work towards those goals, even when you're focused on other tasks at hand. Suddenly, you find yourself with un-tasked time, and you grab a book to not only meet your goals but to also train your brain even further. *Way to go! Way to grow!*

TRAIN YOUR BRAIN: POSITIVITY MATTERS

Believing in yourself is important. Believing in the power

of you is important, too. Remember: *you* are always listening and positivity matters.

When was the last time you said or wrote something positive to a friend, a family member, co-worker, team member? Yesterday? Last week? Within the last six months? Now, when was the last time you wrote something positive to yourself about yourself? Have you ever said something positive to yourself?

Positive aspirations to yourself builds your confidence into a meticulously crafted shield you can use to defend yourself against outside forces. You can use your self-confidence to climb onto a greater stage, make a larger impact in the world, to up level your leadership, and grow even further.

Never underestimate the power of kindness with one another, and never ever underestimate the value of being kind to yourself. Positivity matters. It sets the tone for your leadership, for your team, for your growth. Tell yourself how powerful you are. (*You really are powerful!*) Remind yourself of the greatness you will achieve! (*You will!*) How large and positive your impact on the world will be! (*I cannot wait!*) It is not arrogant to say these things out loud to yourself often; you are training your brain and repetition is key.

Henry Ford once said, "Whether you think you can or think you can't – either way you are right."

Mr. Ford was so right. Why then would you ever want to think you cannot do or achieve something? Don't fulfill a negative self-prophecy! Speak positively about your goals, your to-do lists, your building blocks for success. Train your brain to focus on the possible and the positives!

An easy way to enhance the training of your brain is through your choice of words. Choose positive connotations in your sentences. For example:

Don't forget the milk!

-versus-

Remember the milk!

Don't and *forget* have negative connotations in the first sentence. You are literally telling your brain to forget the milk! Yes, *don't forget* should cancel each other out in the sentence; but your brain won't focus on the "cancellation". It is being programmed to forget your milk. Whereas *remember* adds the milk to your mental shopping list, giving you better odds of bringing milk home for dinner.

Positivity matters even in the words you draw on for your internal dialogue. Choose to speak positively and positive things can and will happen.

Focus on the positive. It is too easy to focus on the negative things in life. You can lose yourself in a vicious circle of thoughts focused on all the negative things you have seen in this lifetime. And if they have gone wrong in the past, they could go wrong again in the future. *Stop!*

Train your brain to *focus on the positive*. Stop being afraid of what could go wrong and think of what could go right. Do not let your fear keep you from living your best life. Do not let the fear of failure keep you from making a positive impact in the lives of others. The 'others' could be people you don't yet know, or they could be your family. *Keep going.*

Do not fear failure. You win and you learn; there is no fail. You either win and learn what works well for you and your team, or you learn how to do better next time. Every game you play, every goal you set, every job you strive to attain – you learn, and you win. Critical growth lessons can be found on your journey to greatness!

Staying positive will not always be easy; there will be grey days. They will happen and this is why training your brain is so vitally important!

On grey days, your training kicks in and you focus on the positivity in life to counterbalance the grey. Even if only subconsciously, your brain will push away the grey and bring positive energy towards you. Focus on the finish line and finding the silver lining in everything you encounter. Speaking positively about your goals, your to-do lists, and your building blocks for success will train your brain to focus on the possible positives and great things will come your way. *Positivity matters!*

FOCUS ON THE POSITIVE

Write down a negatively worded way I used to speak to myself:

Re-write it a more positive, supportive way:

These are two of my favorite aspirations:

MY GOALS

What is one goal I want to achieve this year?

What is another goal I want to achieve this year?

What do I want to attain for me and/or my family?

How do I want to make an impact?

Who do I want to impact?

I've got this!

3

SELF-WORTH: I AM WORTHY

"Your value does not decrease based on someone's inability to see your worth." - Zig Ziglar

---

Self-worth is defined as "confidence in one's own worth and abilities; [see also:] self-respect and self-esteem", and it is important because it influences our decision-making. It can either motivate us to seek our highest potential, or it will underwhelm us and keep us semi-comfortably on the sidelines of life.

Individuals with high self-worth are continuously

reaching for the next level of leadership, the next rung in life, and they are always striving for another goal. This does not mean they're without self-doubt; it means they strive hard and hold themselves in high regard. And if doubt tries to creep in? They focus on the positives in their life and keep their self-confidence fully engaged.

If your self-worth is low, you live and work from the sidelines of life and believe yourself to be quite comfortable. Occasionally, you may experience a desire to grow, but you do not act on it. To me, this is like the old adage about the hound dog on the front porch.

Two farmers are talking in the yard and every few minutes the hound dog on the front porch howls in pain. Finally, the visiting farmer asks, "What's wrong with your dog?"

"He's lying on a nail.", says the owner.

"Then, why doesn't he move?"

"Because it doesn't bother him *enough*."

The hound dog is lying there in occasional pain. It hurts *enough* to make him howl and *enough* to grumble – but it does not bother him enough to get up and move. How much is enough? What is your *enough level*? Are you tolerating a job position because it pays for most things in your life? Does the day-to-day drudgery suck the life out of you *just* enough to keep you wondering but not enough to make you quit? Does it serve your passion in life? Is it enough?

A low level of self-worth can keep you in a lane of life that is only occasionally painful due to a lack of self-growth. You will not leave that lane if life is uncomfortable only every now and then. You are worthy of more than that kind of life! *You are worthy of greatness!*

For my granddaughter's fourth Christmas, I gifted her a book I wrote about her and her favorite stuffed animal friend, Bearemy. They have gone everywhere together since she received him as a gift on her first birthday.

Entitled *Zora Irie and Bearemy©*, the book is chock full of pictures of the adventurous twosome going to random places and familiar spaces; and it is filled with the nonsensical songs we made up at bedtime to talk about their day's adventures. We sing along as we read the book together, and Zora has proclaimed it her "favorite book ever" for more than three years now.

On the very last page of her book, I captured *Zora Irie's Power Words*. Zora has been saying her power words out loud at bedtime since she was two and a half years old. It is magical to hear her say by heart the very things that support her self-worth, growth, and empowerment.

Zora Irie's Power Words

I am smart.

I am kind.

I am loving.

I am strong.

I am beautiful.

I am Zora!

Zora shouts her power words, speaking them into existence each night with a fervent passion! Believing in herself wholeheartedly! Her ending with *"I am Zora!"* solidifies in her growing, young mind the power of being herself. The power of being you. These are power words for certain!

If a young child can believe in the power of herself and find a high level of self-worth, then you can too! It may be buried under years of adulthood or shoved in a corner of your mind because life has tried to get in the way. Whatever the reason or excuse, wake up the power of you. It is important for you and your leadership growth to take stock of just how valuable you are in this life!

Not knowing your self-worth can keep you in the same lane, at the same job, working diligently at something for which you hold no passion.

Let me repeat that: not knowing your self-worth can keep you in the *same* lane, at the *same* job, working diligently at something for which you hold *no* passion. It does not help you grow. You can be a great employee, but a lack of self-worth can keep you from growing professionally. It can keep you from working on your passion.

I want you to know your worth and to know you are worthy.

You are:

Awesome – Unique – Special
Priceless – Worthy – Powerful
Loving – Important – Talented
Strong – Kind – Intelligent

Beautiful – Captivating – Resilient
Passionate – Fearless – Spectacular

What are your Power Words?

I am _____

I am _____

I am _____

I am _____

I am _____

I am _____!

Know your *power*! Know you are *valuable*!

Know your *worth*! Know you are *worthy*!

It is self-respect that helps to define our own worth. Sometimes we hold our heads high, see ourselves clearly, and respect ourselves fully. These are the times our self-worth is high. Why then do we allow others to set a value upon us? To diminish our own self-value?

I believe in you. Do you believe in you? To find and keep a high self-worth value, you must believe in you regardless of what others say about you and, more importantly, what you *think* other people are thinking about you.

I want you to repeat after me:
Other people's opinions about me are none of my business.

Now, read it out loud:
Other people's opinions about me are <u>none</u> of my business.

One more time – out loud – with power!

Other people's opinions about <u>me</u> are <u>none</u> of my business!

That's correct. Unless you are a mind reader *(and maybe not even then)*, what other people think of you is none of your business. Their thoughts are their own and they do not manifest your reality. You do! Your thoughts bring your reality to life!

I believe we would be so utterly disappointed if we knew how little others actually thought of us. We are all so busy worrying about what the other person thinks of *us*, we have little time to give actual thought to *them*.

Get out your cellphone and turn it to selfie mode. Go ahead. I'll wait. Ready?

Now, I want you to look yourself in the eye and repeat after me: *You are worth it. I am worth it.*

Say it again: *You are worth it. I am worth it.*

Say it *three* more times and on the last time, I want you to take a selfie:

You are worth it! I am worth it!
You are worth it! I am worth it!

You are worth it! I am worth it!
[Click!]

Now, pull up the picture. Look at the depth of your smile. Look at how your eyes twinkle with the truth and the genuine pride emanating from you! *This* is what results when you believe in yourself and you know your worth. This is look of worth others see in you, too!

And oh, how worthy you are!

SELF-CARE: IT'S IMPORTANT

Taking action to preserve or improve your own physical and mental well-being is one way to define *self-care*. Self-care is not selfish. Self-care is important, even if difficult.

You may be running, running, and running; constantly helping others; caring for loved ones; stretching yourself thin. You are so busy taking care of others that you do not make time for yourself. But you cannot fill another's cup from your own empty cup. You cannot energize others if you are totally drained. Rest and refuel is vitally important for you and for those you lead at work or home.

You must take an active role in improving, protecting, and enhancing your well-being. Like the repetition we talked about in chapter 2, repeatedly taking care of one's self in times of happiness will train your brain to take self-care action in times of stress, too.

Like any flight attendant will tell you, in times of emergency, you must put on your oxygen mask *first*. Your mask first or you will pass out and not be able to help anyone else. Take care of *you* first to insure you are ready and able to care of others.

Your self-care to-do list is of critical importance to your well-being. Here are a few self-care action examples:

> Breathe. *Relax.* Go outside. Keep calm.
> Enjoy life. Breathe. *Unplug.* Meditate.
> *Be positive.* Have fun! Slow down. *Breathe.*

Sleep is another great form of self-care. Our bodies need to recharge and rejuvenate daily. Give yourself the time you need to refuel your energy tank. You cannot lead wholeheartedly if part of you is always empty, exhausted, and plain worn out.

One of the hardest forms of self-care? *Saying no.* Just because we have an hour free in our day does not mean we have to fill it helping someone else. Planning a relaxing weekend of nothingness when you are invited to join friends at the last minute? If you need a quiet weekend because your energy tank is below empty, say no. Say: that doesn't work for me. Say: Thanks for thinking of me but not this time. Say no because taking care of yourself matters.

There should be no explanation necessary for your friends. We are all adults whose energy and emotional tanks need refueling and rest at different times. Sleep. Breathe. Say no. Repeat, as needed.

Robert Holden says, *"Your relationship with yourself sets the tone for every other relationship you have"*. Now go and take great self-care!

SELF-TALK: *YOU* ARE LISTENING

"Self-talk is the most powerful form of communication. It either empowers or defeats you." ~ Unknown

Self-talk fuels self-confidence and *you* are always listening. What are you saying? About you? About others? You should always strive to positively acknowledge yourself, no negative self-talk.

What does your internal dialogue sound like? Is it a self-defeating *I*, as in *I should have done this or that*? Is it an accusatory *You*, as in *You should have done better*? Remember positivity matters here, too. Evict from your mind the internal critic who is trying to tear you down. Instead, give space to the internal cheerleader who is building you up and supporting your positivity and growth.

Remember: do not say *fake it until you make it*. That tells yourself you are a fake, and your internal critic does not need any ammo. You are evicting that critic from your mind! *Show it until you know it! No negative self-talk!*

Keeping the negative self-talk at bay is an on-going task even for this author. I can be quite critical of myself. One such evening, I was working in the kitchen and muttered something unpleasant to myself.

From the living room, I heard an exasperated scoff in response. To which I paused and took a breath to reply in a liltingly lovely voice, *"Yes darling?"* (HA! Yeah, right!)

As I spun to face him, my actual knee-jerk response was more of a hasty, guttural, "WHAAAAAAAT?!!!"

He took a breath and continued, *"What I know is this: if you ever heard someone talking to your friends the way I just heard you talk to yourself? You'd kick their butt. So be nice! That's my girlfriend you're talking to."*

Awwwww and ouch! The truth can be loving and pointed. My self-talk became a growing opportunity that night.

See how easily your self-talk overflows onto those you love? Make it the kind of talk of which you would be proud. The kind of self-talk that supports and uplifts the person who hears it daily *(Ahem! That's you!)* and the people onto whom it could overflow. Be lilting and lovely to you and them. You all are worth it!

YOU ARE WORTH IT!

Write down something you're tolerating. Something that's not bothering you *enough* to do anything about it for now.

What steps would you have to take in order to change it? (Don't be the hound dog on the porch.)

Rewrite your list of Power Words:

I am _____

I am _____

I am _____

I am _____

I am _____

I am _____!

Give yourself a compliment:

Now another:

C'mon... one more....

Write down a few forms of self-care.

Which one will you do in the next week?

Which one will you do in the next month?

In the next three months?

I am proud of you! You've got this!

4

THE SPOTLIGHT AND THE STAGE

"Pause today and notice something you have worked hard on and recognize yourself for it. Acknowledge your efforts." - Kristin Armstrong

---

At the start of this book, you set your intentions for you how you wished to grow and move through life. You have been working hard throughout this book to train your brain to focus on the positive, and to change not only how you take care of yourself, but also how you speak to and about yourself.

Now, it is time to acknowledge yourself. Besides, how can anyone else in this crazily beautiful world acknowledge you if you won't acknowledge *you*?

Acknowledging yourself means: if no one else is there to celebrate you, you are still there, and you can! Whether it is acknowledging a win in an athletic competition, a great score on a test, a successful compliance review at work, or a job interview that went smashingly well – you did it!

If no one else is there, give yourself a high five. *A self-high five!* Some folks feel silly at first, but that silliness comes from the low side of your self-worth. Positivity matters in everything you do, and you just achieved something spectacular! *You* did it! Now give yourself a high five and acknowledge your brilliance!

Recognize the preparation you put in ahead of the event and acknowledge your hard work. Say it out loud; look at yourself in the mirror; make sure you can hear yourself attesting to your powerful results. It is another beautiful layer of self-talk.

Hearing and watching you acknowledge yourself is important to support your growth not only as a leader, but also as a more empowered, self-confident person. That self-confidence flows through you and will garner recognition from others; ultimately providing you more opportunities to grow in your leadership.

REFLECTION (a/k/a MIRROR TIME)

I am worthy. I am worth it. I've got this!

You need to remind yourself of your self-worth and power whenever and wherever you can. Post-it notes in the car, a bookmark of positive aspirations tucked into your current read, a note taped next to your work phone. Find a way or two or ten to remind yourself of how worthy you are.

I have an easy and powerful way to positively impact your day. To prepare, grab a dry erase marker, a bottle of glass cleaner and a rag. Now head to your bathroom.

Step 1: clean your mirror. This not only gets your medium ready; it also earns you brownie points if you share your home someone else. *(Bonus!)*

Step 2: You and I. You'll need to create two power phrases; one *you* phrase and one *I* phrase. Examples: *I am powerful. You are strong. I am going to make you so proud! You have made me so proud!*

Step 3: write them on the mirror. Write them just above eye level so the mirror can still have its normal function and so it also frames the person looking in the mirror.

Step 4: read the power phrases out loud to yourself every time you look into the mirror. Listen to the truth in each statement. *(Are you actively listening to yourself?)* Give yourself your full attention. Make eye contact with yourself when you read them out loud. Hear and know your power!

Step 5: repeat. Every three days write new power phrases on the mirror. Continue to read them out loud.

Step 6: watch the growth. Notice how you carry yourself in a different manner; how your confidence grows; how less and less you giggle while talking to yourself in the mirror. Notice how you *know the power* of these phrases.

Now, notice how the confidence and empowerment of others in your home grows, too. Once again, the training of your brain and the power of positivity towards yourself is overflowing onto others! What a wonderfully positive impact you are making!

WHERE'S YOUR STAGE?

As a leader your stage is everywhere you are. Whether you are spending time with your family, talking with friends and co-workers, volunteering in your community, or networking at a business event. Seize the opportunity to recognize you are on a stage and you have the opportunity to lead.

Whether you are speaking one-to-one, one-to-two, one-to-ten, one-to-an unknown number because you cannot see the back of the arena, *you* are capable of leading with brilliance! Call on your inner leader, and if you are nervous, perform your way through! Show it until you know it and you will be able to summon your leadership faster and faster each time your stage appears.

When your leadership stage is before you, and you are working one-to-one training a co-worker, how do you shine? You shine by turning the spotlight on the other person; actively listening; empowering the other to be an equally great leader; and by being fully engaged in the happenings on your stage.

Is your stage a fundraiser? Summon your inner leader to showcase the group putting on the event. Advocate for their cause! Shine your own spotlight upon them to help them reach their goals for strategic growth.

What if your stage was at home? Empowering the next generation of your family is legacy-building. How do you support their growth? Through actively listening to their dreams and aspirations. You can also help them identify their passions in life and be a great cheerleader as they strive toward their own goals. Shine the spotlight on them so they can shine bright!

As for the spotlight: you're welcome to step in at any time. If you do not want the spotlight on you, that is ok, too! Then, take the controls of the light and shine it upon someone else. *You are a leader even if they cannot see you.* You are shining as a leader even when you are illuminating another. *Shine on, Leader!*

What if others cannot see you but they can hear you? Reach out and direct a project through conference calls; or support the personal development of others through podcasts. *You can be an influence even if they only hear you.*

Near or far, your ability to positively impact a situation

or person is limitless! By now, I hope you know I believe in you and your abilities to help others grow. Do you believe in you? Because you absolutely should!

Write down four things for which you deserve acknowledgement.

Write down a few power phrases for your mirror and beyond.

Where are your [leadership] stages?

If you don't want to be in the spotlight, identify others you can help shine:

Shine on!

5

MINDSET MATTERS: BE H.A.P.P.Y.

"I should probably warn you I'll be just fine... Because I'm happy." - Pharrell Williams ®

Of all the positive-focused activities you do in life, *choosing joy* should be chief among them. When presented with any number of circumstances, what happens when the outcome is unknown? I hope you choose joy and choose to be happy. Taking the journey of life with joy as your companion makes for happier 'travels'.

I know. I hear you. *"It's not that easy, H."*

Trust me. I *know*.

And yet I still say, when you cannot see your destination because of the mountain before you, choose the path that is lit with joy so your journey may be ripe with happiness. The path may still be full of obstacles, potholes, and detours that delay you in reaching your destination... but at least your route is illuminated with joy. *Keep going – you've got this!*

So, how do you find the joy?

Be H.A.P.P.Y...

HARMONY: ARE YOU IN SYNC WITH YOURSELF?

Mahatma Gandhi said, "Happiness is when what you *think*, what you *say*, and what you *do* are in *harmony*." Harmony is your inner balance between life and your surroundings.

Are you in sync with yourself? Or are your day-to-day actions grating against the vibrations of harmony within? Are you working against yourself? Meaning, are you doing something for others that goes against your principles? Saying one thing but doing another? How are you staying in harmony with yourself? Out of harmony can equal unhappy and no one wants you unhappy. *(Least of all me if we can help it. Right?)*

Finding your harmony keeps *you* in balance with your life and ultimately with your leadership, too. Not letting a grey day negatively impact your work or your family relationships takes dedication to keeping your harmony steady. Being true to your own principles and staying in balance.

ATTITUDE IS MINDSET AND IT DOES MATTER

Your attitude sets the tone for happiness. And you will be exactly as happy as you decide to be or decide *not* to be. *(There is no question.)*

Positive mental attitude (PMA) is a mindset of having an optimistic outlook when encountering anything in your life; and this positive outlook will attract positive energy and positive outcomes.

PMA is a practice that takes effort and focus, and while it is not always easy, it *is* a habit worth building. This mindset keeps you focused on the positive and your brain training will keep your subconscious seeking positive results. Positive mental attitude also means you will find a way to reach and attain the goals you have set for yourself, and not an excuse to keep you at the starting line.

If you are mid-point on a project, and the results are looking mediocre at best, pause. Re-evaluate. How can you reach a positive outcome? Recalibrate, reset the players, and *go!*

Stay focused on reaching the end with your best results.

Even if your path changes in the middle of your journey – keep going and stay positive!

PREPARE YOUR SURROUNDINGS AND YOU

Robert H. Schuller said, *"Spectacular achievement is always preceded by unspectacular preparation."* Prepare and preparation. While quite possibly boring, they are excruciatingly necessary steps when striving towards success.

To paint a room, you would never simply buy the paint and start slapping it on the wall. You would first prepare the room by covering or removing furniture; taping the edges of the room to protect trim work; gathering your supplies; and asking for help, if needed.

For the best results, preparation is key!

Preparation + Opportunity = Success. If you see an opportunity in the distance, do not immediately start chasing it down. You would not leave your chair with zero minutes of training and go run a marathon. You need to prepare yourself to achieve this goal.

Prepare yourself with power words, positive mental attitude, and hard work. Let's say you're seeking a new job position. You would prepare for the interview by studying the company and their strategic goals. How do they give back to the community? Are you aware of their company culture? Their reputation as employers? Devise a plan for your interview including questions to ask the interviewer(s) and be ready to slay the day!

Just like training to cross a marathon finish line, preparing your surroundings – both physical and mental – will help you achieve a goal of happiness and joy. If you do not prepare and plan for your happiness, the negativity and the sorrow of the world will try to creep in and squash your joy. Stay focused on the positive!

Remember: *you* choose how happy you will be.

PURPOSE AND PASSION

Live with purpose. When you find your purpose, you will not need to chase opportunities or people, they pursue you! The energy of intention brings to you those opportunities. Remember intention? You set your learning intentions at the very beginning of this book. Setting your intentions with your life, your goals, your work brings the things you are seeking unto you.

In December 2015, Bob Goff, a two-time New York Times Best-Selling Author and philanthropist, tweeted, *"We won't be distracted by comparison if we're captivated with purpose."* So true!

Stopping to compare yourself to others robs you of your positive mindset. Do not look at others to determine if you are on the right path. Live with intention and *be you*.

Being the best possible you is one layer of your purpose. How do you find the rest of your purpose? Can you identify it? Not certain? That's ok.

"If you can't figure out your purpose, figure out your passion. For your passion will lead you right into your purpose."
~ Bishop T.D. Jakes

So, what is your passion? Is there anything that you do today that fills and excites every fiber of your being? How do you serve? What gives you joy? What invigorates you and encourages you to do more and dream even bigger? *Find your passion!* Whatever you decide to do, make sure it brings you joy!

Seek your purpose *within* your passion. Meld the two together and BOOM! You are a world-changer making positive impact everywhere you go! YES!

YOU. JUST BE.

Yes, it is that simple: just be you. Take my teachings and grow from you or add to you; but at the core still be *you*. I want you to take the knowledge you need or want from this book, tomorrow's conference, or next month's podcast, and be the best possible you. The world needs *you*.

Grow with the tips and tricks from this book and the books of many other brilliant authors and leaders, but the core of you should still be *you*. With your intentions, your vision, your goals – *be you*.

Be happy. Be free. Be joyful. Be yourself. Be awesome! Do not try to fit yourself into a preconceived idea of what *you* think *we* think *you* should be. Nonsense! Be. you.

Be you and the world will adjust!

Keep yourself in harmony. Set your attitude. Remember your PMA. Prepare. Plan. Find your purpose. Set your intention. Choose happy. Choose joy. *Be* happy. *Be you!*

Is there anything you are doing that is not in harmony with yourself?

What will you do differently?

What is your purpose?

What is your passion?

What gives you joy?

Be you and the world will adjust!

6

IT'S SHOW TIME!

"I'm watching it come true... Oh, this is the greatest show!"

- Justin Paul and Benj Pasek ®

Congratulations! You have reached the end of this guide and it is show time! It is time for you to step onto the stage and begin your greatest show of leadership.

Before you step into the spotlight, let's review key elements of confidence-building from this book:

- Effective, two-way communication is one key to great leadership and success. Success for your team members. Success for your co-workers. Success for your company. Success for *you*.

- Lead by your willingness to change and engage your audience. Assess yourself and calibrate. You still need to be you. It is the delivery of your presentation, or talk, the leading of your meeting – *that* is what you can recalibrate.

- Show yourself just how capable you are of shining even on the greyest of workdays. Show your team what a great leader acts like during times of heavy work. Work hard, carry your part of the workload, and show your leadership. Show you are a great leader until you *and* they know it. Because there will be days of burdensome, heavy work but there will be an even great number of days full of amazing joy, triumph, and success!

- *Speak your goals out loud – even if you can only whisper right now.* You are still listening. Remind yourself of your goals and how important they are for you and the impact you wish to make in the world. Remind yourself *often*.

- Believing in yourself is important and believing in the power of you is important, too. *Remember: you are always listening.*

- Train your brain to *focus on the positive.* Stop being afraid of what could go wrong and think of what could go right. Do not let your fear keep you from living your best life. Do not let the fear of failure keep you from making a positive impact in the lives of others.

- Self-worth is important because it influences our decision-making. It can either motivate us to seek our highest potential, or it will underwhelm us and keep us semi-comfortably on the sidelines of life.

- A low level of self-worth can keep you in a lane of life that is only occasionally painful due to a lack of self-growth. You will not leave that lane if life is uncomfortable only every now and then. You are worthy of more than that kind of life! *You are worthy of greatness!*

- It is self-respect that helps to define our own worth. We must hold our heads high, see ourselves clearly, and respect ourselves fully.

- I believe in *you*. Do you believe in you? You must believe in you regardless of what others say about you and, more importantly, what you believe other people are *thinking* about you. Say it out loud: *Other people's opinions about me are none of my business.*

- You cannot energize others if you are totally drained. Rest and refuel is vitally important for you and for those you lead at work or home.

- You must take an active role in improving, protecting, and enhancing your well-being.

- Evict from your mind the internal critic who is trying to tear you down. Instead, give space to the internal cheerleader who is building you up and supporting your positivity and growth.

- *You are a leader even if they cannot see you. You can*

be an influence even if they only hear you.

- Stopping to compare yourself to others robs you of your positive mindset. Do not look at others to determine if *you* are on the right path. Live with intention and *be you*.

Be you and the world will adjust!

As you grow, and up level your leadership, remember to shine like a bright beacon of joy, radiating positivity to everyone who can see you. Show it until you *and* they know it. If you are practicing your mirror work and believing in yourself *(I've got this!)*, you will radiate joy to *you*, too!

Joy is contagious – spread it around! *Shine bright!*

Show it until you it! Be you! Exude joy even if you must show it until you know it somedays. Because the grey days will try to squash your smile and steal your joy; keep shining! Be a leader through and with your joy. *Shine bright!*

Even if people try to reject you, shine on! As artist Lady Gaga once said, *"Do not allow people to dim your shine. Tell them to put on some sunglasses."*

Keep shining! Be your brilliant self! Show it until you

know it because soon enough you *will* know it and so will everyone else!

I believe in you! Don't stop! Don't quit! Never give up! Love yourself with *immense* joy! Be fierce! Be you! You have absolutely got this!

You <u>are</u> a leader and now you *know* it. More importantly, *now* is the time to show it.

I believe in you! *Now, go get it...*
~H.

WITH GRATITUDE

Show It Until You Know It would never have been finished without key people in my life.

Thank you to my dear friend, Allison Liddle, who taught me how to launch into my own next level of leadership. Thank you for the lunch that led to so many new life chapters! I promise to *Keep Going!*

Thank you to my editor and dear friend, Karen Nerison, for her keen eye and loving, frank opinions. You also brought my virtual life to reality and I am immensely grateful. *Woot! Woot!*

When I disappear into my writing cave, the world around my keyboard can fade away because Jason Witt is at the helm of our time ship. He reminds me that self-care is critical and that his girlfriend *(that's me)* deserves great things in life. Thank you, MOTAS, for loving me always and for being my personal roadie, too. *I love you.*

Thank you to my first-born granddaughter, Zora Irie, for showing me legacies are gifts from the universe. I am in awe of your intellect and beauty and I am immensely proud to be your Gigi. Thank you, my Z-girl, for the joy you bring! *I love you with all the hearts! Happy New Year forever!*

Thank you to my children, Arianna, Walker, and Aurora, for being three of my greatest gifts in life. As your Momma, I strived to share my life's lessons with you. Instead, you were the teachers. Thank you, my Beloveds. I am proud of all of you and love you immensely!

Thank you to my mom, Jewell, and my stepdad, Tom, for all of their support. *I love you.* As a sister to many brothers, I thank them all for the precious gifts of my nieces, Kalie and Harper, and nephews, Caleb, Easton, Lucca, and Matteo. *Auntie H loves you all immensely!*

When I was little, I prayed every new year for a sister and I was finally blessed with soul sisters when I was old enough to appreciate them. Thank you to my BFF Soul Sister, Michelle Huber, for being my release valve and life enabler. *(Free Your Mind and Jive Bunny forever!)* Thank you to my Soul Sister, Christine Ellis, for being a phenomenal friend, always ready for a road trip karaoke and a dose of life harmony. *(Let's get it started – and never stop!)*

To my family, *framily*, many other soul sisters, and friends who supported and loved me: thank you all.

To my readers: I will continue to believe in you. *You've got this!*

with fierce love, ~H.

THE PLACE OF H LLC

theplaceofH.com

www.ingramcontent.com/pod-product-compliance
Lightning Source LLC
Chambersburg PA
CBHW070209100426
42743CB00013B/3106